30 DAYS TO STOP SUCKING START THRIVING

GET YOUR MINDSET IN CHECK

JESSICA LEWIS

MASCOT BOOKS

MASCOT BOOKS

www.mascotbooks.com

30 Days to Stop Sucking, Start Thriving: Get Your Mindset in Check

For more information, please contact:
Mascot Books
560 Herndon Parkway #120
Herndon, VA 20170
info@mascotbooks.com

Library of Congress Control Number: 2017903491

CPSIA Code: PBANG0417A
ISBN: 978-1-68401-249-7

Printed in the United States

30 DAYS TO STOP SUCKING START THRIVING

GET YOUR MINDSET IN CHECK

JESSICA LEWIS

INTRODUCTION

WHY WAIT??? Start living the life of your dreams NOW!

The path that God has led me on has taught me many of the mindsets I will share with you in this book. At 19, I quit school and started as an independent life insurance agent at World Financial Group. There, I excelled quickly and made significant income in my early twenties. I developed discipline and habits that allowed me to make over $450,000 in income before my 25th birthday. From there I met my husband, Skylar, and we created a marketing company that thrived in Carlsbad, California. That company was taken over by our management staff, which freed us to start another company in the water damage restoration industry, Superior Restoration. With God's blessing, we have turned that company into a multi-million-dollar business that prides itself in its great service to our customers and employees.

With more than ten years of business experience, I then went out on my own and created Success with Jess. Success with Jess is a coaching company where I personally help people max out and take each area of their life to the next level. I do everything from speaking to large companies to conducting medium-size workshops and working one-on-one with people. My hope is that this book inspires you daily as if I were there with you, encouraging you and showing that we all have the same hang-ups and struggles. As you go through this book, please reach out if you need support. My email is Jessica@successwithjess.org.

Oftentimes we go through life just "doing." Few people spend time reflecting and purposefully planning their lives. Those that do rarely execute those plans. This book will help you find your dream life that has been waiting for you to show up.

Each day, you will be given a topic and questions to help you discover your truths and reflect on your thoughts around it. Topics will include: goals and what you want, thoughts you do not realize you think, how to deal with thoughts that do not serve you, habits that successful people practice, how to break down your goals, and much more.

For best results, get a partner or group of people together and go through this book together. Read and journal on one chapter per day. Some chapters build on the subsequent ones, so I recommend reading it from front to back. Allow yourself to be honest and open to discovering new things about yourself and others. The truth is not always exciting or easy; however, the only way to have a breakthrough is to first breakdown. Everyone will have a different experience, but my hope is that you all learn to love and connect with what matters in your life and begin acting on those things immediately. In 30 days, you will have discovered what you want out of life, what is currently stopping you from getting there, and what you need to do and think about differently to achieve it.

It's time to step into the greatness God created you for!

MUCH SUCCESS,

Jessica

TABLE OF CONTENTS

DAY 1 - THE LIFE OF YOUR DREAMS

"Where there is no vision, the people will perish."
– Proverbs 29:18

Almost everyone knows the power of goal setting, yet few of us consistently do it with laser focus. Knowing of something intellectually and knowing of it from experience are two completely different things. As I work with and coach countless people, most do not have a clear, concise, measurable, or inspiring plan for their lives. They have no clue where they are going. Instead, they are just going through the motions. Most of their actions are based on how they feel each day, rather than a purpose greater than themselves that is pulling them to act, even when they don't feel like it.

If you could create the life of your dreams, what would it look like?

I am not talking about just any goals. I am talking about what you were born for. Why do you exist? Why were you put on this planet?

If you don't know what your big picture looks like or how your goals for this year move you closer to your long-term plan, they can easily become just another year's goals. Year after year it can become just another plan. If you have a clear, concise, motivating plan of what you were born to become, inspiration comes easier. Motivation comes easier. The days of not feeling like doing something become less common. Your emotions do not dictate your actions.

Who would you have to become, what would you need to have, and what would you have to do to feel that you have lived your life with no regrets?

Imagine a life where you do everything you want to do. You have what you want to have. You are fulfilling your God-given purpose for existing. You're at the top of your game, you're maxing out, you're in flow, you're making things happen.

What would the ideal version of you look like, feel like, talk like, walk like, smell like and be like?

For some of you, desirable characteristics may include impactful, powerful, excited, happy, grateful, joyous, connected, passionate, etc. If you were free to dream big without holding back and allow your truest desires to come forth, what would life look like?

No restrictions. No filters. What would those desires be? Who were you born to become? Why were you put on this planet?

Who do you want to become?

What do you want to BE?

What do you want to do?

What do you want to have?

What do you want to create?

DAY 2 - BEAUTIFUL LIARS

"You must learn a new way to think before you can master a new way to be."
– Marianne Williamson

Our brains are so intelligent that we can convince ourselves of anything. We are great at gathering evidence for the things we "believe" to be true. We see things through the filters of our beliefs, which are created from our past experiences, primarily from our childhood.

Science proves that most of our beliefs and patterns of thinking are formed before we become teenagers. We do not consciously form our beliefs; this happens subconsciously. At critical moments in your childhood, you unconsciously made decisions about your view of the world and life. This led to the formation of your beliefs. Most people never revisit where their beliefs and patterns of thinking came from. They just spend their whole lives believing them to be true.

When I was 5 years old, I remember going to a dinner celebration that everyone was very excited about. It was when my father that raised me had legally adopted me. I remember not being that excited, but went along with it anyway. I hadn't thought about the event for years. Then, as an adult doing some soul searching, I realized that I was very angry about that day. I realized that day was the day my dad decided he did not want to be in my life. At 5 years old, how can you process that? It was the day he signed his rights over as a father and gave them to my new dad. It was the day I felt abandoned and betrayed. In that moment, as a 5-year-old child, I created a story and made up a belief about who I was and what that event meant.

From every event that occurs in your life, you create a story of what it means about you. At one point, for me it used to mean that I was not good enough to be loved. It used to mean I didn't deserve to have a father who loved me. As I grew older, it naturally turned into a story that I did not deserve to have a man that loves me. Is that true? H-E-L-L NO! Did I believe it as truth until I was aware of it? YES. That one belief that I was unaware of led me down a path of never being able to feel and accept love from men. It was not possible. I believed my own story: that I was not loveable.

There are numerous events that have happened in your life that have caused you to form your beliefs about yourself. Some of them serve you, some don't. The good news is that those stories can be changed if you become aware of them and create new ones.

Today we are going to look at those "stories" that don't serve us. We have been saying many of them for too many years. These stories are ones that limit us. They come up when we are about to step out of our comfort zones, do something new, take risks, or have the potential to be hurt. It's the still, small voice in our head that tries to convince us why we can't, why we aren't good enough, why we aren't the right size, shape, etc. These stories prevent us from reaching life's full potential by turning into our limiting beliefs.

When you write out a huge income goal and the still small voice in your head says...

When you want to connect with God on a deeper level and then think, *but I am…*

When you finally find the relationship that could be "the one" and you start telling yourself...

When you want to get that big promotion, or leave your job to follow your passion, or go up to that guy/girl who's super-hot and talk to them, or when you're going to try something new and that voice says….

Some of these voices may be saying things like you're not smart enough, you're overweight, you don't deserve that, only successful people can do that, you're not good enough, there's not enough time...

Write down 10 of your stories that limit you.

1. ______________________________

____

____

____

2. ______________________________

____

____

3. ______________________________

4. ______________________________

5. ______________________________

6. ______________________________

7. ______________________________

8. ______________________________

9. ______________________________

10. ______________________________

Be aware as these limiting stories come up throughout the day. Truly see how silly some of them sound and how utterly untrue they are.

DAY 3 - THE ROOTS OF THE FRUITS

"If you want to change the fruits, you will first have to change the roots. If you want to change the visible, you will first have to change the invisible."
– T. Harv Eker

Where did these limiting stories come from?

Where did all your beliefs come from?

They come from many places:

- Parents
- Grandparents
- Teachers
- Friends
- Movies
- Media
- People of influence
- Mentors
- Pastors
- Babysitters
- EVERYWHERE

Can you begin to see that what you have believed to be true is not actually true?

Take a deeper look at the limiting beliefs you wrote yesterday and begin to ask yourself when and where you adopted that belief as truth.

In your childhood or early adulthood:

What event(s) happened where you felt stupid? In that moment, what did that event mean about you? What story did you tell yourself about who you were?

____

____

____

____

____

In what event(s) did you feel powerless to change, no matter how much you wanted to? In that moment, what did that event mean about you? What story did you tell yourself about who you were? What story did you tell yourself about others?

What event(s) happened where you were denied love? Heart-broken? Or felt unlovable? In that moment, what did that event mean about you? What story did you tell yourself about who you were? What story did you tell yourself about others?

What event(s) happened where you were embarrassed? In that moment, what did that event mean about you? What story did you tell yourself about who you were? What story did you tell yourself about others?

What event(s) happened where you felt stupid? In that moment, what did that event mean about you? What story did you tell yourself about who you were? What story did you tell yourself about others?

When have you felt abandoned? Or completely alone? In that moment, what did that event mean about you? What story did you tell yourself about who you were? What story did you tell yourself about others?

What situation has made you the saddest? Or the most disappointed? In that moment, what did that event mean about you? What story did you tell yourself about who you were? What story did you tell yourself about others?

When did you feel that you couldn't do something? When did someone tell you that you couldn't do it? In that moment, what did that event mean about you? What story did you tell yourself about who you were? What story did you tell yourself about others?

When did you feel you were not good enough? In that moment, what did that event mean about you? What story did you tell yourself about who you were? What story did you tell yourself about others?

This is not the time to go into a pity party. This is the time to suck it up. You are good enough, smart enough, strong enough, and capable enough.

Be gentle on yourself, and I challenge you to revisit this as time goes on. It took me years of soul searching to remember the day that I was adopted. I buried it so deeply that I did not remember it at all. Then one day it came to me and everything got a lot clearer. There is freedom in knowing.

Answer the questions above today and for the rest of your life.

DAY 4 - TESTING OUR THOUGHTS

"Perspective is the way we see things when we look at them from a certain distance and it allows us to appreciate their true value."
– Rafael E. Pino

In one of my all-time favorite books, *Loving What Is* by Byron Katie, the author walks you through a series of questions to see the truth in the thoughts that we think. She makes you aware of how these thoughts affect you. Thoughts arouse emotions of happiness, joy, anger, frustration, empowerment, hate, love, etc. Do you have control over those emotions, or do they just seem to happen? Katie has shown me that I can choose to be angry if it serves me. Before doing her work, I would just BE angry, without choice. Do you just react sometimes and wish you had more control over the emotion you feel?

I have read numerous books on how to control my thoughts and what thoughts to think. They helped make me aware of thoughts when they come up, but all were missing one important part: what to do when they get past my awareness and take control of my emotions.

Today we are going to dive into what to do when these thoughts that do not serve us arise.

When I say thoughts that do not serve us, I am referring to the ones that cause an emotional reaction that doesn't serve our life purpose or positively impact us.

My summary does not give full justice to the subject that Byron Katie dedicated an entire book to, but it will begin the journey and enhance your awareness of how your thoughts affect you.

EXAMPLE: Write out a statement of how something makes you feel and why. For example: *"I am angry with my husband because he doesn't pick up his clothes."* Then answer the following questions based on that statement. Example in italics for each question. Answer for yourself as well.

Is it true? YES OR NO.

Yes, I am angry.

Can you absolutely know that it is true?

Can I absolutely know that I am angry that he doesn't pick up his clothes?... Well, not absolutely. I am probably angry about multiple things. So, NO.

How do you feel when you think this thought?

I feel angry, frustrated, and impatient. I feel like he does not care for what I want and he just wants me to be his maid and pick up all his stuff as he drops it everywhere. (Definition of feelings: an emotional state or reaction).

How does thinking this thought cause you to act toward yourself and others? Be specific.

I get distant and cold and do not connect with him. This ends up hurting me as well as him, because I shut him out when I am angry. I am not happy when I am angry. I am not as productive when I am angry. I dislike myself when I am angry.

Who would you be without this thought? How would you act differently without this thought?

I would be free, careless, happy, joyful, and loving. Overall I would be much happier.

How might you act differently if you no longer thought this thought?

I would just pick up his clothes or leave them there for him to pick up. No stress. Happy. Joyful. My usual self.

Does this thought (the original statement you wrote) cause you stress or peace?

STRESS.

Knowing how this thought makes you feel, would it serve you more to drop it or keep thinking it?

Drop it.

As you go through these questions, pay close attention to how you feel when you think the thoughts and who you would be without them.

When I go through these questions, I often find that I no longer wish to feel that emotion and CHOOSE to feel something different. I often find that my brain reacts before I can logically think it through and CHOOSE how I want to react. These questions have given me the tools to take control over my reactions and CHOOSE how I will respond to any situation. I hope they do the same for you.

Use these questions today and any day you think a thought that causes you frustration, anger, or any emotion that does not serve you in becoming better.

DAY 5 - GOD MADE YOU PERFECT

"Perfection is seeing everything that isn't perfect and allowing it to be perfect."
– Jessica Lewis

You were made perfect. A newborn child can do no wrong. Most people feel love, compassion, happiness, joy, excitement, etc. when they see a newborn baby. So why is it that when you see an adult you do not get those same feelings?

Children are tenacious, relentless, persistent, focused, loving, accepting, caring, carefree, brutally honest, and much more. Everyone loves babies. Babies bring people joy and happiness. They remind you of everything that is good, innocent and pure. Babies can do no wrong. No matter what, you lavishly pour your love onto and into them. At some point in life, that feeling of love seems to stop. When did you stop loving yourself and others the way most people love babies? When did you stop seeing the greatness, purity, innocence and beauty in yourself?

Something shifts as you begin to experience life. You get hurt, disappointed, lied to, cheated on, let down, abused, made less than, and bruised.

I am here to tell you that all those experiences you have been through, including the ones you hide and keep secret, have made you into the person you are today. They have driven you to do the things you have done. Any good or great thing you have done may not have happened if you had not experienced the challenges that you have. All experiences contain blessings if you are willing to see them.

I can now say that I am grateful for my biological father letting my dad legally adopt and raise me. At one point, that was one of the most painful memories I had. Now I realize that I would not be the person I am today without that experience. I choose to feel grateful for that experience. I wouldn't want it any other way. My entire life, I have felt that I must prove to people that I am good enough to be loved. That has led me to be a successful businesswoman with the tenacity and spirit to succeed.

Typically, people can remember the negative, hurtful and painful times in their lives much quicker than they can the exciting, amazing, and joyful ones. Today's exercise is meant to make the muscle of remembering the positive qualities about yourself stronger. I want you to rekindle the love that you have for newborn babies for yourself. I want you to see yourself for the amazing person that you are.

Write down 10 of your best qualities:

Write down 10 things you are good at:

Write down 10 reasons why you are amazing:

If this was a difficult exercise for you, I challenge you to repeat it regularly. Build the muscle of knowing the positive things about yourself and make it stronger than the muscle that knows the negative things you are not proud of.

If this exercise was easy for you, I challenge you to assess whether you are using these traits to their fullest potential. Are you maxing out every single day, stepping into your greatness, and blessing the world with your gifts? If you are not, how can you start today?

DAY 6 - VICE GRIP

"No amount of guilt can change the past and no amount of worry can change the future."
– Unknown

Shame, blame and guilt are powerful emotions. They keep you in bondage if you do not shed light on them and allow yourself to be free. You carry the shame, blame and guilt from your past with you everywhere you go unless you make a conscious choice to STOP.

Shame, blame and guilt make people feel less than, unlovable, unhappy, depressed, and yucky! They keep us in a state of feeling undeserving, unworthy and undesirable. Today you are going to break the chains and allow yourself to be free. You cannot go into the past and change your choices, actions, or behaviors, but you can choose how you feel about those situations. Every experience you have gone through up to this point has molded and shaped you into the person you are today. There has been something positive from each experience.

I know some of you are saying, "But life would have been a lot better without those experiences." I hear ya! But can you really know that is true? Does it serve you in any way by thinking that? Or does it make you feel hopeless? It is delusional to wonder how life would have turned out without our experiences, because they have already happened. We cannot change our past, but we can change how we think about our past. We can change the story we tell ourselves about the past.

Today we are going to gain perspective on these experiences. We are going to look at all sides and not just see the negatives. Some of you may need some support with this. We have told ourselves the same stories for so long, so at first it may be difficult at first to see it another way. However, if you're ready, you will. It is possible.

1. Make a list of the times you have felt shame, blame or guilt.
2. Write out how that experience served you and anyone else involved in a positive way.

EXAMPLE: A mother on drugs got her kids taken away.

Positive for her: She could fulfill her immediate desires at the time and do drugs and get high.

Positive for them: The kids formed an unbreakable closeness with their grandparents and were out of the presence of drugs and a mom that was unable to care for them.

Is this true? Absolutely. Will you want to hear it? Maybe not. I challenge you to go there. There is a positive in every situation if you are willing to see it.

Be extremely aware of your self-talk. Would you have liked the situation to never have happened? Of course! Did it? Yes. So, knowing that you cannot rewrite the past, how did it serve you and the other people involved?

If you are having trouble thinking of how it was positive for you or someone else, give yourself some space and come back to it. There is always a positive to it. It just may take you a moment to see it.

Write out a time you felt shame, blame, or guilt:

How did the experience serve you and everyone else involved in a positive way?

Write out a time you felt shame, blame, or guilt:

How did the experience serve you and everyone else involved in a positive way?

Write out a time you felt shame, blame, or guilt:

How did the experience serve you and everyone else involved in a positive way?

Write out a time you felt shame, blame, or guilt:

How did the experience serve you and everyone else involved in a positive way?

DAY 7 - PLEASING EVERYONE EXCEPT WHO MATTERS MOST...YOU

"Freedom comes from true choice that honors you."
– Jessica Lewis

Most people unconsciously do things that they think they "have" to do, "should" do, or are "supposed" to do. Your beliefs of what you "have" to do, "should" do, or are "supposed" to do come from your childhood experiences, your parents, and other influential people over the course of your life.

They sound like: (You fill in the blanks)

A wife should...

____

____

____

A husband should...

____

____

____

Kids should...

____

____

____

My parents should...

____

____

____

I should....

____

____

____

I shouldn't….

____

____

____

He should….

____

____

____

I am supposed to….

____

____

____

You are supposed to….

____

____

____

A spouse is supposed to…

____

____

____

As I have become more aware of the dialogue I have inside my head, I have begun to question myself more. Some things that pop up that I feel I "should" do or that my kids or husband "should not" do are ridiculous. I laugh at myself sometimes. I often also say, "Who the heck made up these 'rules' of things I 'should', 'have to' or 'must' do?" I sure didn't.

For example, one of my beliefs that I have battled with is that a wife should stay at home with the kids, and that this shows she loves them. Is that true? No. Can my kids still feel loved even if I am not a full-time stay-at-home mom? Yes.

My husband should always kiss me goodbye before he leaves. Should he? Who says so? I may say so, but if he doesn't do it then maybe he shouldn't.

My 4-year-old should not throw rocks. I heard myself say that and then asked, "Is that true?" No, I don't think so. As long as he isn't throwing them at people or cars, who cares if he throws rocks? He's a child.

Kids should be seen and not heard. Is that true?

People should show up to meetings on time. Who says that? Do they?

Just because you believe something should happen a certain way, does it?

Some of your beliefs are bogus and you do not realize it.

Some of these beliefs are for the approval of others. A great indicator that I am doing something I think I "should" for the approval of someone else is when I am extremely drained after doing it. I wrestle with not wanting to do it, and go back and forth over and over, exhausting myself.

There was a situation where I did not invite a certain relative to a party. It was my party and I did not want to invite them. Then one of my parents said, "But you have to invite them or else they will get upset." At a prior point in my life, I would have done it because I needed their approval and did not want to upset them, even though I did not want them there. I would have done it because I thought I "should." I would do it to avoid conflict. But when it happened this time I said, "No, I am not going to invite them. It is okay that you think I should, but I am not going to." I stayed true to myself and did not alter my actions because of my desire to be liked and approved of by them. I was okay with any conflict that was going to arise. I did not give in to what they wanted; rather, I did what I felt I should do, and was willing to own any outcome that resulted from it.

No one that did anything great was liked by everyone. It isn't possible. You cannot be influential, take a stand, or create huge success without someone disagreeing with you. I know this truth. Yet I often find myself doing something I think I "should" so that I do not inconvenience, anger, or frustrate someone else.

Write down the things you do because you think you "have" to, "should" do, or are "supposed to."

With yourself:

____

____

____

____

With your spouse:

____

____

____

____

With your kids:

____

____

____

____

With your parents:

____

____

____

____

With your relatives:

____

____

____

____

With your friends:

With people:

At work:

With your goals:

With your career:

With your emotions:

DAY 8 - PASSION

"Passion is an excitable energy that will carry you to your dreams if you let it. Today, don't stuff it away or shut it off. Let it run free for everyone to see."
– Jessica Lewis

It is easy to be in a routine of just living to get by. Or just doing the minimum to stay afloat.

Remember when you were a child and had huge dreams? You were going to be a firefighter, a cop, an astronaut, a difference maker, a doctor, etc. You were going to do something huge! Huge! There was nothing that was going to stop you. You didn't tell yourself any "stories" about how hard it was going to be. You didn't tell yourself any "stories" about how you couldn't do it. You didn't get discouraged at anything. You were unstoppable. YOU HAD NO FEAR.

If you are honest with yourself, life may have just happened. Based on your decisions and awareness at the time, you ended up in the job you "thought" you should do, the career that makes the money you need, the career that fell into your lap, the career that was convenient, the career that your parents would be proud of, etc. Bottom line, most people are not in the career of their dreams. Why? Where did you get the idea that you could not be passionate about what you do and make money? How long are you going to settle for just getting by?

What if you were working in the field of your passion every day?

What if life wasn't where you just ended up?

What would life look like if you were in your dream career?

Maybe it isn't just a career, maybe it's every area of your life. Whatever you have passions for: a hobby, a relationship, a place, traveling, etc.

Today is the time to rekindle your passion and get your juice back. What was the passion you had as a kid, when failure wasn't even in your consciousness? The passion you had when you did not drag the disappointments, discouragement, frustration and failures from past experiences into the present moment? Imagine the place where fear is not present. The place where you are unstoppable, invincible and nothing will get in your way. What would your life look like? In all areas, what would you be doing?

Answer these questions as though you have a couple million dollars in the bank and life's necessities are taken care of. Do not answer from what you "should" or "ought" to do.

What are 5 activities that energize you?

What are you passionate about?

What do you love doing?

How often are you engaged in doing these things?

How can you begin doing 2-3 of these activities NOW?

Act on one thing today and plan the rest out so they will all be started in the next 3 months.

DAY 9 - TRUE CHOICE

"The 3 C's in life: Choice, Chance, Change. You must make the choice to take the chance if you want anything in life to change."
– Anonymous

Now that you know what activities energize you, how are you going to incorporate them into your life? Do you want to stay in the status quo? Or do you want to know that when you die, you can honestly say you maxed it out?

Being aware is Step 1.

Acting is Step 2.

It is not enough to have an awakening for a couple of moments, a day, or even a week. Our brains are wired so strongly that it takes years to undo and reprogram our patterns of thinking and habits. I am not saying it is impossible. This is simply a warning, as we are creatures of habit. We need to set reminders for ourselves to ensure we are moving toward what drives us.

Examples of how we can stay on track:

Spend time with peers that you're vulnerable with and that know your "true" passions and challenges.

Create written reminders and goals that you read regularly.

Have an accountability system or a partner.

Email me about coaching programs I have available at:

Jessica@successwithjess.org.

Set daily reminders on your phone.

ACTION Steps:

To move yourself closer to fulfilling and living your passions, list what you are going to:

Start: ____

____

____

____

Stop:

Continue: (by your choice, rather than because you think you "have" to, "should", or are "supposed" to)

What would life feel like if you did everything from true choice?

DAY 10 - BEGINNING WITH THE END IN MIND

"Every morning you have two choices:
Continue to sleep with your dreams, or wake up and chase them."
– Unknown

What is your life goal that you want to achieve to change the world? What impact do you want to make? What do you want to be remembered for?

Sometimes we live our lives like we have all the time in the world. You know you're in this category based on how focused you are. People that are on point and clear on their personal missions do not spend hours in front of the TV. They do not get consumed with social media, on checking out everyone's business. They do not go through the day and let the distractions sway them. They do not let weeks go by without growing, stretching, or progressing in some way.

Do you approach your life like you will be around forever?

Life for me moves fast. It seems like the years keep getting faster and faster. I focus daily on maxing out the precious time that God has given me. We rarely watch TV at our house; we do not pay for TV services. I have no clue when we would fit it in. When I am home, I am with my husband and my children. I am present, aware, and focused on them. When I am at work I am there, present and focused on work. Every week I am growing and moving my life forward towards my life mission, because I am clear on what I want my life to look like when my time is up.

Answer the following questions:

If you were to die today, what would you want read at your funeral?

____

____

____

____

____

____

What do you want to be known for?

What kind of person were you?

Who and what did you impact?

Are there a lot of people there? Who?

Would they say you lived your life to the fullest?

What will you be remembered as and for?

What was your mission statement?

DAY 11 - BHAG

"Impossible is just a big word thrown around by small men who find it easier to live in the world they've been given, than to explore the power they have to change it. Impossible is not a fact. It's an opinion. Impossible is not a declaration. It's a dare. Impossible is potential. Impossible is temporary. Impossible is nothing."
– Unknown

Are you great at keeping secrets? We keep secrets about things we are not proud of, things that bring us shame, things that could ruin our reputation, and things that we wish we would have never done. Ironically, we also keep secrets about our biggest dreams and aspirations. Most people have a huge goal that they feel is so out of reach that they do not share it with anyone.

I would venture to say that moving your crazy big goal from your head to paper is a crucial first step in achieving it. It is impossible to know you have arrived if you do not know your destination. The first step I always take to accomplish a goal is writing it out on paper. I am not certain what exactly happens, but when I write a goal or vision on paper, it instantly begins to become more real to me. The impossible becomes much more possible.

The definition of intention is "a thing intended; an aim or a plan." In my experience, I may not know how some things are going to happen, yet once I get clear on what I want to have happen, things just begin to fall into place. I am often scared to write my biggest goals down because my limiting stories convince me that I am not good enough before I can even get them on paper. For example, one of my huge goals is to be a $1,000,000/year paid speaker and coach by the time I am 40 years old. We have a thriving water and fire restoration company that provides for our amazing lifestyle, but I am going to create a second career that impacts people even more. As I got clearer on that goal, I wrestled in my head with it because I am not positive about the exact steps to achieve it. I still am not clear. One thing I am clear of, though, is that I am on my way.

What is your BHAG?
AKA, your
BIG
HAIRY
AUDACIOUS
GOAL?

It is the goal that is so scary you don't even say it out loud. Not many, if any, even know about it. You keep this one all to yourself.

Well today, let's let the cat out of the bag.

What is the scariest, hairiest, biggest goal you want to accomplish in the next year?

____

____

____

____

____

____

____

____

____

What is the scariest, hairiest, biggest goal you want to accomplish in the next 5 years?

____

____

____

____

____

____

____

____

____

____

____

What is the scariest, hairiest, biggest goal you want to accomplish in the next 10 years?

I would love to support you along the way to achieving your BHAG. Send it to my personal email at Jessica@successwithjess.org to share it with someone who will see you achieving it.

DAY 12 - WHY WAIT? THE TIME IS NOW

"Waiting is your way of not taking a risk and staying in your comfort zone. No one ever waited and did something great. Pansies wait. Champions get it done. What are you waiting for?"
– Jessica Lewis

I often find myself waiting for things. Waiting for the right timing. Waiting for the kids to get older. Waiting for myself to get older. Waiting for my husband to get it started and I will follow. Just waiting.

I think it is ingrained in us from childhood. Go to school, get a good job, work hard, save money. Then when you retire, you can travel, be free, enjoy yourself, etc. etc.

Well, I am here to call BS.

I call BS on having to wait because you're not old enough. I was 20 years old when I owned my first insurance office, making a multiple six-figure income.

I call BS on waiting until all things are perfect to move into your dream house. Within 3 weeks, my husband and I moved out of our perfectly gorgeous property to fulfill our dream of living on the beach.

I call BS on having to go to school to make a great living, where you can have freedom to be with your children and spouse. We have structured our lives so that we are free to come and go, yet still provide for all our wants and needs, and neither of us graduated from college.

I call BS on waiting to travel until you get older. If most people saved the money they spent on eating out or Starbucks, they could travel every year.

Today, get clear on the things you want to experience in life that you are waiting for and decide not to wait any longer.

What are 20 experiences you want to have in your lifetime?

____

____

____

What are 1-5 that you can make happen within the year?

Which ones can you make happen in the next 5 years?

Could you get the entire list done in the next 10 years?

DAY 13 - THE NITTY GRITTY

"Setting goals is the first step in turning the invisible into the visible."
– Anthony Robbins

We have found that when we have clear outcomes, we achieve them; however, the problem lies in not consistently setting the outcomes.

When setting goals, we use the SMART system below.

S- Specific (The clearer our target, the easier it is to hit)

M- Measurable (Is it trackable?)

A- Achievable (Stretch yourself)

R- Risky (What makes you uncomfortable to say out loud?)

T- Time (When will it be accomplished?)

For example:

A goal that sounds like: I want to be healthier.

Is it specific? Not really, what does healthier mean?

Is it measurable? No

Is it achievable? Sure

Is it risky? Not sure

Is there a time in which it will be accomplished? No

As you set each goal, go through all five questions for each one. Get in the habit of using these criteria so that you set yourself up for success.

1 Year from Today

What accomplishments will you have created in the following areas:

Spiritual Life

____

____

____

____

____

____

Giving Back

Volunteering

Influencing others

Other

DAY 14 - EXPECTATIONS DRIVE RESULTS

"I'd rather risk expecting the best and be let down, than hope for the worst and be surprised."
– Jessica Lewis

It is possible to have it all in life. Our expectations drive our results. The problem is, most of the time we don't take time to set our expectations, or we set them too low. There's a saying, "Don't expect things to happen. It is better to be surprised than be disappointed." I strongly disagree. I want to set an expectation and goal that I can live into, not one that I am already living.

If you could create anything you desired, what would the following look like:

Relationship with yourself:

____
____
____
____
____

Relationship with significant other:

____
____
____
____
____

Relationship with kids:

____
____
____

Relationship with siblings:

Relationship with parents/grandparents/parental figure/person you look up to:

Relationship with friends:

Relationship with coworkers:

Other:

What is one thing you could do that would make the biggest impact on all your relationships?

DAY 15 - WHETHER YOU FEEL LIKE IT OR NOT

**"Do not wait to strike until the iron is hot;
but make it hot by striking."
– William B. Sprague**

God has blessed me with extraordinary success in business. Doors were open to me and I took massive action. Opportunities are always in abundance around me.

Part of the reason I feel I have been given so many opportunities is my willingness to do whatever it takes. I am willing to do what others will not. When I was in the financial services industry, I was relentlessly consistent. I was in the office before everyone and left long after they all went home. I consistently did the things that created results over and over and did not stop. Most people do it for a little while and then they stop. Starting and stopping takes much more energy than just staying consistent in the first place.

When my husband and I started a marketing company, I worked on my close and phone pitch day and night so that once someone called, my pitch was so strong hardly anyone would say no. When we started our restoration company, I cut drywall, cleaned carpets, knocked on doors, and did whatever it took to get the business going. Even if you don't know the way, take action. It is easier to make improvements and adjustments when you are in motion. Do not wait to figure it all out to start. By the time you figure it out, your strategy will need to be updated and you will never get started.

I was clear on what I wanted and why I wanted it. Those things drove me to take action even when I didn't "feel" like it. Feelings do not have a chance to bring me down because I have trained myself to act before they take me over. There are only two ways you can be: in action or not. When I am not in action, it is easier to be fearful. If I am fearful, I become paralyzed and taking action takes 10 times the effort than what it had to.

What is going to drive you to do things you do not feel like doing and to stay in action?

1 Year from Today

What accomplishments will you have created in the following areas:

(Continually using SMART system)

Business/career:

Side business: (if applicable)

In order to accomplish the goals you listed what do you need to:

Start:

Stop:

____

____

____

____

____

Do more of?

____

____

____

____

____

DAY 16 - SHORT-TERM PLANNING TO ENSURE LONG-TERM SUSTAINABILITY

"Stamina is the force that drives the drumming; it's not really a sprint."
– Neil Peart

As I have worked with people over the years, it seems that as human beings, we tend to be able to focus on one area of our lives extremely well and if we do not intentionally plan the other areas, they will get left behind. For example, when I was in the financial services industry, I was great at working all day long every single day. I was so focused on my work and prioritized it so much that all other areas of my life fell off the map. I slowly gained 40lbs over the course of 5 years. My relationships were minimal or non-existent. What I did not realize at the time was that if I did not take care of my body, I wouldn't have the energy to sustain my intense work schedule.

Not only did my energy decline from neglecting my body, but my confidence declined as well. My self-esteem sunk to an all-time low. I was so focused, I never let myself have fun. I always was on. During the times when I had opportunities to be relax, I was physically present yet mentally in my business. It got so crazy at one point, I won a free trip to Hawaii for 5 days and I did not go. I wanted to stay home and work. Madness, right? Who would turn down something like that?

What I have found after resetting from that experience is that if I take care of my body while being extremely focused, I do not burn myself out as quickly. I learned that life and business are about the journey, not just the destination. Of course, we all have times of intense focus where life will be out of balance. There are seasons in everything.

Today we are going to check your physical goals. It's important to set yourself up for long-term success and wellbeing so you can crush it, year after year, with no threat of avoidable health problems or loss of energy.

6 Months from Today:

What accomplishments will you have created in your physical fitness?

How will you physically push yourself to the next level in six months?

1 Year from Today:

What accomplishments will you have created in your physical fitness?

How will you physically push yourself to the next level this year?

DAY 17 - REVERSE ENGINEERING

**"We are what we repeatedly do.
Excellence, then, is not an act, but a habit."
– Aristotle**

One of the pivotal keys that has led to success in both my business and my personal life is my daily habit tracking. To make a huge goal attainable, it helps if you break it down into smaller steps. Take a large goal and figure out what you need to do every day to achieve it. I use my daily activities to track my progress and know how close I am to completing my goal. Doing that took away my discouragement and fear. It made my goal seem attainable and I was clear on what I needed to do. Clarity gives you faith. With faith, you act. With action, you get results.

For this to be most effective, you will want to know your numbers, ratios, and closing percentages. You may not know these in the beginning; do not let that stop you from starting to track and reverse engineer your goals.

For example, if you are in sales and you want to make $100,000 this year:

That is $8,333/month and $2,083.25/week.

Depending on how your income is generated the scenario will vary, so work with it.

The thing I would want to know or guess in the beginning was how many sales it would take to hit the numbers above.

EX: If each sale I made averaged $1,000, I would need to make 8.3 sales in a month.

Then I would want to know how many appointments it took me to make a sale.

If my closing ratio was 25% I would need to have 4 appointments a week on average to make one sale. If I needed to make 8.3 sales a month to hit my goal, that meant I would need 4 x 8.3 = 33.2 appointments to hit my income goal...

Next, I would want to know how many calls I needed to make to set 1 appointment. If I knew that, then I would know exactly how many calls I needed to make to get my 33.2 appointments. For example, if it took me 2 calls to set one appointment, then each month I would need to make 2 x 33.2 = 66.4 calls to hit my income goal.

Then I would want to know how many people I would have to talk to in order to get enough leads for a viable prospect to call and book an appointment with.

If you follow that pattern, you can find out exactly what you need to do daily to hit your annual goal.

Even if you do not know your exact numbers, use your best estimations and adjust as you go.

This will take a huge goal and reduce it down to the daily things you will need to do to hit it. It makes each bite easier to swallow.

For example, I knew that to recruit 4 people a month, I had to meet 5 new people a day and make 25 calls. If I did that every day, it would yield me 4 new people joining my business. Once you know your numbers, the key is doing them every day. Day in, day out. Repeatedly. Consistently.

For each area of your life, reverse engineer what you need to do daily to ensure you hit the goals that you set.

Spiritual

____

____

____

____

____

____

____

____

____

Relationships

____

____

____

Business/Career

Physical

Begin to track your activities closely and adjust your daily habits as needed as you see your patterns emerge.

This will give you an opportunity every day to stay on track towards hitting the large goal you set for the year. The big becomes small. Every day is an opportunity to reset and do better than the last.

DAY 18 - CONSCIOUSNESS IS CONTAGIOUS

"Energy is contagious, positive and negative alike. I will forever be mindful of what and who I am allowing into my space."
– Alex Elle

We have all heard the saying that sounds something like, "You are who you surround yourself with." Or, "You are the sum of the 5 closest people to you." For some of us, this is a scary statement. We don't even like the people that we hang around the most. Some of you are hanging around unmotivated, angry, frustrated, unfulfilled, or negative people.

Are you intentional with the people you surround yourself with?

If you are like my husband and me, you consciously seek out and find friends that are growing and moving like you. We have outgrown some friends and limited ourselves with others. Not that we are better than anyone, because we are not. We all came from the same creator. But we understand that consciousness is contagious. We have chosen to be around people that have the same moral, ethical, and growth-oriented beliefs. We surround ourselves with people who are willing to be real and get vulnerable.

This is something I recommend you continually revisit. If you are constantly growing in different areas of your life, you'll always need and want different associations.

What are 5-10 qualities you want in the people that you spend time with?

Which friends have these qualities?

Which friends do not have these qualities?

Who are you going to spend more time with?

Who are you going to spend less time with?

DAY 19 - GREATNESS LEAVES CLUES: THE NEXT LEVEL OF ASSOCIATIONS

"A mentor is someone who sees more talent and ability within you than you see in yourself, and helps bring it out in you."
– Bob Proctor

Do you find people more experienced and successful than you and learn how they achieved their success? Or do you grind it out and make all the mistakes on your own?

I have had the experience of doing both. When I was younger and had lower self-esteem, I did not feel I was deserving of people's time. I had many mentors that were willing to show me the way, but I did not maximize their support. I would act and figure it out on my own. Sound familiar?

I tend to be an introvert. When I think of reaching out to people and asking for support, the unworthy part of my brain turns on and starts going crazy. It sometimes convinces me of all the reasons I should not call. It says things to me like that person is busy, I can figure this out, this is such a small problem so why should I ask for help, etc. Sounds convincing, right? Logically, it makes sense. What I have found is that when I do reach out, my questions lead to something else and then something else and I gain tremendous insight. My small questions lead to a mentor asking more questions and uncovering beliefs that are getting in my way.

Either approach works. One is a long road full of learning lessons that potentially could have been avoided. The other is full of learning lessons as well, yet hopefully many that can be navigated better, quicker, faster or avoided altogether.

Some of the most inspiring conversations come from people that are doing the same or better than me in an area of my life. Greatness leaves clues. I follow those clues and implement them in my life. Do you?

Once again, finding mentors or coaches is an intentional action. It is not something that happens on its own. It will take you being vulnerable and reaching out for support, fellowship, coffee, lunch, or anything to get together. You know you're moving in the right direction when you go to call someone and you get that uncomfortable feeling in your stomach.

Who are your current mentors?

Who do you want your mentors to be?

Who do you need to be or become to attract better mentors into your life?

DAY 20 - PIVOTAL PIECE TO YOUR PUZZLE

"One good mentor can be more informative than a college education and more valuable than a decade's income."
– Sean Stephenson

I am forever grateful to have a confident, smart, and emotionally intelligent husband that is working on himself at the same time I am, because I can bounce ideas off him and get feedback. I am not always open to receiving the feedback as soon as it is given, but eventually I come around and internalize it.

I have noticed that I am not open to feedback when I am in a high emotional state. When emotions are high, my logic and reasoning tend to be low. When my emotions are low, my logic and reasoning are high. For example, when I am angry or frustrated and my husband tries to give me feedback, I resist him. I fight back and do not want to hear what he has to say, even though he is usually right. I am in it. Immersed. Fully present to my feelings. I must allow myself to calm down or break my state to internalize any logic. At the beginning, getting out of your heightened emotional state may be difficult; it may take you a couple of hours to calm yourself down to be logical, but as you practice and become more aware of yourself you will get increasingly better at it.

My husband and I have the type of relationship where I can share my deepest fears, regrets, and thoughts that do not serve me. Most of the time, those thoughts are ridiculous and my fear is getting the best of me. It helps to have him to snap me back to my senses and make me recognize that I am talking nonsense to myself. It's good to have people in your corner that you can share those deep feelings with, who will lift you up and shake you to your senses. Make sure that person is someone who will always have your best interests in mind. You do not want to rely on someone that will be jealous, envious, or too focused on themselves.

We also have a coach so that we are not the only people having those tough conversations with each other. I want to preserve my closeness with my husband and not be his boss, so a coach is a great middle person. He helps us see our gaps and potential areas of improvement. So, if it isn't your spouse or a coach, make sure that it is someone, or several people, who can act as a mentor or mentors. You may consider having someone in multiple areas of your life. Find people who you can have vulnerable conversations with, who have the strength and wisdom you are seeking to gain. A trainer that is in great physical condition for your body, a coach for business that has done what you're trying to do, a person who is great at relationships to help you get better, or someone who is stronger in their faith than you are.

What are 5 things that stop you from achieving your goals?

____

____

____

____

____

____

What steps are you going to take to ensure they don't get in your way this year?

____

____

____

____

____

Who are you going to enroll to support you in your specific goals and dreams for the following areas?

Faith

____

____

____

____

____

Family

Fitness

Finances

DAY 21 - THERE IS NO STABLE: ARE YOU GROWING OR DYING?

"Non-progress is the killer of pursuit."
– Jessica Lewis

My chief goal in life was to get into a place where my life was stable. My world was rocked when I discovered there is no such thing as stable. You are either growing or dying; there is no in between. One of the words that comes to mind for me on this topic is homeostasis. I thought this was when the body was stable. The definition states that homeostasis is "the tendency of the body to seek and maintain a condition of balance or equilibrium." It is not when something has achieved that balance, but the "seeking to maintain" the balance. Life is constantly in a state of flux and there are always things happening and changing.

I previously thought that if I had a certain amount of money in the bank, I could relax. Then I could be free from worry. Then I would be good. Well, what happens if the market crashes? If things change? If I change? Thinking that once you hit or attain something and at that point everything will be good is a delusion. We do not know what the future has in store. All I can seek to control is my present. Changing my thinking this way has allowed me to handle changes in my life much better. I adapt and change faster, allowing me greater opportunities, income, healing, and much more. I would not have discovered this life-changing concept if I was not open to growing and becoming better.

Are you growing or dying?

Each year are you getting better, or staying the same, AKA slowly decaying?

What is your growth plan for the year?

How many books are you going to read?
(When planning them, what intentional areas are you going to improve in?)

What seminars, workshops, courses or conferences will you attend this year?

What new skills will you begin?

What new skills will you master?

DAY 22 - PERCEPTION & CONTROL

"Forgive yourself for not knowing what you didn't know before you learned it."
– Unknown

Everyone is doing the best they can at every given moment. Do you believe that?

Let's say you mess something up and wish you had done something different. Doing something different in that moment was not possible, or else you would have done it.

We all operate at our current level of awareness and we are doing the best we can. There is no other way. If you do not agree with the actions or attitude someone else has, there is no reason to resist it; they made the best possible choice they could have in that moment. That is hard to swallow for some people you know because you want them to be different. Do you ever want someone to act, think or be like you? Because your way is best? You want them to react like you. What makes you think your way is best? It is not possible for them to act/react differently until they become aware of why they act like they do and have a desire to do something different. Our reactions are subconscious and happen before we have a chance to process them. You telling them to change will not cause them to change. They must become aware of their actions and consciously choose something different in that split moment of decision.

We all see things through our "filters." Our "filters" are made up of our past experiences, hurts, failures, times of joy, sadness, pain, etc. It is unrealistic to think everyone that will react exactly how you would when they have had different life experiences. Based on their "filters" and their perceptions, they are reacting in the best way they possibly can. It could not be any other way.

Who are you trying to change?

____

____

____

Whose actions do you not like or disapprove of?

Who do you need to let be themselves?

Who are you trying to control?

How much extra energy would you have daily if you took your focus off of trying to change others and channeled that same energy toward achieving your goals and dreams? What could life begin to look like?

DAY 23 - VICTIM VS RESPONSIBLE

"The greatest act of courage is to be and own all of who you are– without apology, without excuses, without masks."
– Debbie Ford

When a situation happens and you get hurt, it is easy to point the blame finger at someone else and see how they should have done something differently. It is easy to be a victim of your circumstance.

When you are a victim, things are continually happening to you. Outside circumstances determine your experiences. You do not have any control of anything. The opposite of being a victim is choosing to be responsible. You can choose to acknowledge that you have a part in every experience that you encounter. You can choose to see things from a different perspective and know that you are contributing to every experience that comes into your life.

If you got in an accident, you chose to drive the car. If you are in a bad relationship, you have chosen to stay there. If you are overweight, you have chosen to eat the food that you did. If you are unhappy, you have chosen to be that way. This is not always an easy thing to accept, so today we are going to start with the grudges that we have. When we have a grudge or resentment against someone else, it is typically because a situation occurred that you thought should have gone differently. You are victim to the experience. Until you can acknowledge your part in the experience, you will always remain a victim to it.

Seeing things from someone else's perspective forces us to drop our egos and open our minds to being forgiving, even when we are hurt. Loving, even when we are angry. Seeing the good, even when it all feels bad. Even potentially being wrong. It is not always an easy process, yet isn't it better than staying angry, hurt, and feeling bad? I do not know about you, but I want to do what serves me best in the long term more than I want to be right. I have a big ego, but I also realize that my way is not the only way. I do not always have to be right. I do not always have to be in control. It is a higher level of consciousness to recognize that you can choose to be the victim or you can choose to be responsible and see things from another point of view and how you played a part in the situation.

Think of the person you resent, are angry at, or have the most negative energy on, and answer the following:

What happened to cause you to feel the way you do?

What did you want them to do differently?

What are a couple of reasons they may have acted reacted the way they did?

Are there any experiences from their past that could have potentially played into their reactions?

____
____
____
____
____
____
____
____
____

From a responsible place (you contributed to this event happening), what part did you play in this experience?

____
____
____
____
____
____
____
____
____

What could you have done differently?

____
____
____
____
____
____
____

Repeat daily as needed.

DAY 24 - WHO IS THE "REAL YOU"?

"Your life will be transformed when you make peace with your shadow. The caterpillar will become a breathtakingly beautiful butterfly. You will no longer have to pretend to be someone you're not."
– Debbie Ford

You have a side of you that you hope no one will ever find out about. I am talking about all the secrets that you do not tell anyone, A-N-Y-O-N-E. Even the people closest to you don't know what they are. They are the things we have done, said or thought that cause us shame or guilt. Things you were not proud of. Things you wish you could undo.

The great thing is, we all have things like that. The even better thing is that there is healing and freedom in sharing those secrets. It takes a lot of energy to keep things to yourself. Many people think that one cause of disease and cancer is from the unreleased energy we have on situations, people and things. The things we ball up and hold onto. When I am angry and I acknowledge out loud that I am angry, I somehow begin to feel better. Women are probably very familiar with this. They talk to their friends about their problems and afterwards they feel much better. No great advice was needed; they just needed to say it out loud. It releases something in us and makes us free.

Part of having unconditional love for yourself and others is acknowledging and accepting the things that you have done that you are shameful of, embarrassed about, and wish would have never happened.

Once you begin to accept the entirety of you—the good, the bad, the ugly—you can begin to experience unconditional love for yourself and others. Only when love yourself fully will you be able to love others fully. Guys, I am not leaving you out of this one. I know you have insecurities and shameful secrets that you hold onto as well. Do not skim over this and think it is not for you. It is for us all!

What are 10 things you are not proud of, ashamed of, or have never told anyone?

Who is someone you could share some of these with?

Do it, then write down the feeling you experience once you are done.

DAY 25 - DIGGING DEEPER

"Healthy habits are learned in the same way as unhealthy ones– through practice."
– Wayne Dyer

Are you aware of the walls that you keep up to make sure people do not get too close? I keep people at a distance so that I do not have to be vulnerable or in a position where I could be hurt. I do this subconsciously and consciously to protect myself. In doing it, I miss out on deep and vulnerable connections. I miss out on truly expressing my authentic self, and others miss out on getting to know the real me.

I love meeting people who are comfortable in their own skin. Comfortable being imperfect. Comfortable with their flaws. Comfortable and accepting of absolutely everything about themselves. You can sense when someone is confident without being cocky, certain yet inviting, easy to connect with and accepting. I am not there 100%, but I am on my way. When you meet with someone, do you allow yourself to be vulnerable and share the true you? Or do you pretend to be interested in things you aren't and act different than who you are? Most of us act different. We want to be accepted. We want to be loved. Acting different than who you truly are doesn't allow you to have depth in your relationships. They have no choice but to remain superficial.

You know if you go deep with people based on the types of conversations you have. When you are at lunch with someone, what do you talk about? Do you talk about other people? Do you talk about negative things? Do you talk about positive things? Do you both vent about your significant others? Do you talk about your boss? Is the conversation uplifting and motivating, neutral, or draining? Is the conversation about real struggles that you are having? Or is it all peachy keen and you are perfect?

Do you talk about things that make a difference and matter?

Do you share things that are vulnerable and uncomfortable?

Choose a relationship you want to improve:

How can you go deeper?

What can you accept about them to allow you to connect deeper?

Do they know the real you?

Do you know the real them?

What's your vision for your relationship?

DAY 26 - MODELING

"Children learn more from what you are than what you teach."
– W.E.B. DuBois

As we have discussed prior, how we act, our patterns of thinking, habits, and behaviors were learned from our parents, grandparents, parent figures, teachers, coaches and friends. We learned how to live, love, care, act around others, be happy, be sad, grieve, etc. from everyone else. Some people say they don't want to be like their parents, yet it is inevitable and they find themselves more and more like them every day.

As I become more aware of myself, I notice how much I am more like my mother than I had realized. I avoid conflict. Guess who I got it from? Yep, her. I used to avoid any type of situation where I could potentially inconvenience anyone. I would rather go out of my way and spend time doing something myself than inconvenience someone or ask for support. This keeps me safe. It keeps me relying on myself. No one can let me down if I do not ask anyone for anything. Nothing can happen if I do not ask anyone for anything.

My parents had a turbulent relationship at times. One of the emotions I was familiar with was my mother having anger. Guess what my go-to emotion is? You guessed it: anger. I am quick to go to anger. It is not a conscious choice; rather, it is subconscious pattern I had repeated over and over. Even for silly things like stepping on my toe, I become instantly angry and am ready to attack. When I step on my husband's toe, he feels pain and that is it. Me, I am pissed.

Another area we tend to model after our parents or parental figures is our marriage and/or our intimate relationships.

We are either similar or we do the exact opposite. If that is the case, at some point we decided that we disliked someone's behavior so much that we will not be anything like them and go to the opposite extreme. My father was very unaffectionate and I sought out a husband that was nothing like him. I am married to the most loving, accepting and affectionate man ever, the opposite of my father.

What did your primary caregivers model for you in their relationships?

With friends?

How was your mother or female figure? How did she act? What was her typical mood? How did she interact? How did she love?

Do you see any of those qualities in how you act?

How was your father or male figure? How did he act? What was his typical mood? How did he interact? How did he love?

What traits/habits do you see that you have gotten from them?

What traits/habits are you doing the exact opposite of?

DAY 27 - MONEY

"Money treats you the exact way you treat it."
– Jessica Lewis

There are many different opinions about money. Money is by no means the most important thing in life; however, the lack of it makes life difficult to live. My relationship with Jesus and serving him is the most important thing in my life. The more money that I create, the greater influence and opportunities I have. The greater income I make, the more money I can tithe and change lives with. Your relationship with money will determine how it treats you.

Some love it.
Some hate it.
Some are good with it.
Some are bad with it.
Some it leaves quickly.
Some it stays with.
Some use it.
Some lose it.
Some like it.
Some make it.
Some take it.

What is your relationship with money?

Does it stay with you, leave fast, come quick and leave quick, non-existent?

How were you parents or parental figures with money?

How were your grandparents with money?

What traits did you pick up from them?

In regards to money, what would you like to:

Start:

Stop:

Continue:

DAY 28 - YOU

**"My primary relationship is with myself–
all others are mirrors of it."
– Shakti Gawain**

Your relationship with yourself will dictate the depth of your relationships with others. If you do not love, accept, or truly embrace your whole self—the good, the bad, the ugly—no matter what someone else does, you will never be able to feel their love, acceptance and kindness.

In the days of my husband courting me, we had a very direct conversation around this topic. He was extremely caring, understanding, supportive, kind, and much more. He was everything that I had wanted in a man. Yet, there were many times I expressed that I felt he didn't love me. He could have done absolutely everything perfectly, yet until I could start loving myself, I was not able to feel his love. This man would bring me flowers weekly, massage me nightly, take me to exotic places, and was the most thoughtful person ever, and somehow I could convince myself that I did not feel love. MADNESS!

It's funny how we are so nice, caring, loving, understand, and gentle with everyone but the people closest to us, especially ourselves. I have been majorly guilty of this one. No one had to criticize me because I was my worst critic. I am harder on myself and those closest to me than I am on other people.

How do you treat yourself? Are you patient, kind, loving, encouraging? Or are you your worst critic, hard, impatient and mean?

If you wanted to win the love of your soulmate and you treated them the way you treat yourself, how would they feel about you?

Now, stop beating up on yourself. Take a deep breath. Thoughtfully answer the next couple of questions.

In regards to loving yourself, what are you going to:

Start:

Stop:

Continue:

DAY 29 - GRATITUDE

"The most intoxicating, life altering drug: GRATITUDE."
– Jessica Lewis

It's all a matter of focus.

When I am in a bad mood my husband will often ask me, "What are you focused on?" Often, I am concerned with things that do not serve me, things that are not going the way I want them to, things that I am bothered about, or things that are just plain negative.

Once I am willing to answer his question, he then asks me, "What are you grateful for?" Gratitude has a way of erasing all my negativity. How can I be in a bad mood when I think of all the countless blessings that I have in my life? I know there are many people in worse situations than me, so I have nothing to complain about. Gratitude is the ultimate state changer.

This next exercise is about embracing and moving your focus from what is not working to what is working.

What are 20 things that are going well in your life?

What are 20 things that you are grateful for?

Add this to your list of things that you do daily. If you can stay in a grateful place, the sky's the limit to what you can do, be, have and feel.

I challenge you to repeat this exercise the next time you are depressed, grumpy, angry, or in a poopy mood. LIFE CHANGING!

DAY 30 - SOME-A-DAY...

"One person's craziness is another person's reality."
– Tim Burton

My family and I recently moved to the sands of Newport Beach. Any "bucket list" of mine always had that on there. We were going to live on the beach. Each summer, we would rent a beach house right on the boardwalk to experience a small piece of what we wanted our life to be like every day. There was nothing between us and the sand except the sidewalk. The sunsets were uninterrupted. The waves were directly in front of us. It was our slice of Heaven on earth.

At one point, this was the ultimate dream for me. I thought we would have this one day, just not right now. When we get older and have saved more money, then we will do it. When the kids are out of the house, then we will do it. When this. When that. When, when, when.

One day I got a wild hair and said to myself, "What are we waiting for?" We lived in what was then our dream house. We were starting the final project to make the house exactly how we wanted it. We had painted, redone floors, kitchen counters, and bathrooms, landscaped outside, automated most of the house, decorated perfectly, and were about to finalize the master bedroom. My amazing husband agreed to look at places on the beach with me and weeks later, we moved into an ocean front home.

It happened that fast. It was amazingly powerful to see how I made all these reasons and excuses for it happening later in my life when the entire time it was just a choice. We all make choices like that every day. We are waiting for the perfect timing. Waiting for a certain scenario. Waiting. Waiting. Waiting.

What are you waiting for that you are not going to wait for anymore?

What is your dream that can be a reality NOW if you choose?

If you had 30 days to live, what would you do?

ACT NOW

CONCLUSIONS

A vision without action is a dream. Now that you have clarity on where you want to go, who you want along with you, what is no longer going to stop you, how amazing you truly are, and what your relationships are going to look like, the next thing is to start acting.

We can plan all this stuff out, but if you do not do something TODAY, NOW, RIGHT AWAY, you are at risk of slipping back into your typical routine; this would have only been an interesting 30 days that gave you clarity for a moment before it quickly faded. Do not let that happen. Take action.

Review what you have written from the last 30 days. BEFORE you get overwhelmed, take a deep breath. The world doesn't change in a day. Stay in the land of abundance and possibility, keeping any negative self-talk down to a minimum. Focus on the pages with your goals that you want to accomplish this year.

This is not going to be an easy road, but who said it was supposed to be?

"Winners are not afraid of losing, but losers are.
Failure is part of the process of success.
People who avoid failure also avoid success."
– Robert Kiyosaki

If you need support, reach out.

If you need someone to hold you accountable, find someone.

If you get started and then stop, start again.

If you want a coach, email me at Jessica@successwithjess.org

Don't be the person who talks a good game, has it all figured out, then does nothing.

Oftentimes, people do things that are the easiest. We leave the thing that we do not want to do until the end of the day and then happen to never get to it because we were so "busy." It is not okay to avoid doing the things that you do not want to do because they are uncomfortable. That will not create success in your life.

Tackle the most important things first in your day and let them empower and fuel you to do the others. The energy you create from pushing past a barrier is contagious. This will be a pivotal key to you collapsing timeframes and doing things faster. An accountability partner would be of great value here. Whether it's us or someone else, you will need support in moving past barriers and reaching new heights you have not yet hit.

Lastly, I would be doing you a disservice if I didn't mention that none of the success that I have created in my life could have happened without my blessings from God. If Jesus did not come to this earth and die for my sins, I would have much less hope and faith than I do. I would have been doomed to Hell. But our marvelous creator changed our destiny and took the penalty of our sins and died for us. Because of Jesus Christ dying on the cross, I have faith and know that I am going to Heaven. I am forgiven. I am made whole again. He gave me all my great qualities, all my ambition, and everything that is good in me. I have a different level of faith in everything that I do because I know where I am going when this life is over. It is priceless to know that I am going to Heaven when I die. Everything I do in this life will not be in vain. I strive daily to use all the gifts God has given me and step into the greatness that he created me for. If you want that same hope when you die, an understanding that you will go to Heaven, then repent, ask Jesus into your life, and welcome to the family.

"You don't always see the progress you make but every page you read, every call you make, every rep you do, every push you make, makes a difference. They all build on each other to create the you you're striving to become. Squeeze as much as you can, as fast as you can, as quick as you can, and magic happens."

– Jessica Lewis

To schedule Jessica for a speaking engagement or
Stop Sucking Start Thriving Workshop go to:
Successwithjess.org/speaking

For Coaching Questions and Inquiries go to:
Successwithjess.org/coaching

Connect on Social Media

FACEBOOK: https://www.facebook.com/jessicamarielewis/
INSTAGRAM: https://www.instagram.com/jessicamarielewis7/
LINKEDIN: https://www.linkedin.com/in/thejessicamarielewis/

Success with Jess